The City of Ember

Jeanne Duprau

TEACHER GUIDE

NOTE:

The trade book edition of the novel used to prepare this guide is found in the Novel Units catalog and on the Novel Units website. Using other editions may have varied page references.

Please note: We have assigned Interest Levels based on our knowledge of the themes and ideas of the books included in the Novel Units sets, however, please assess the appropriateness of this novel or trade book for the age level and maturity of your students prior to reading with them. You know your students best!

ISBN 978-1-56137-064-1

Copyright infringement is a violation of Federal Law.

© 2020 by Novel Units, Inc., St. Louis, MO. All rights reserved. No part of this publication may be reproduced, translated, stored in a retrieval system, or transmitted in any way or by any means (electronic, mechanical, photocopying, recording, or otherwise) without prior written permission from Novel Units, Inc.

Reproduction of any part of this publication for an entire school or for a school system, by for-profit institutions and tutoring centers, or for commercial sale is strictly prohibited.

Novel Units is a registered trademark of Conn Education.

Printed in the United States of America.

To order, contact your local school supply store, or:

Toll-Free Fax: 877.716.7272
Phone: 888.650.4224
3901 Union Blvd., Suite 155
St. Louis, MO 63115

sales@novelunits.com

novelunits.com

Table of Contents

Summary 3

About the Author 3

Background Information 4

Characters 4

Initiating Activities 5

Vocabulary Activities 5

Ten Sections 6
    Each section contains: Summary, Vocabulary,
    Discussion Questions, and Supplementary Activities

Post-reading Discussion Questions 19

Post-reading Extension Activities 20

Assessment 21

Scoring Rubric 31

Skills and Strategies

Comprehension
Sequence, inference, prediction, compare/contrast, cause/effect

Literary Elements
Genre, plot, mood, theme, irony, figurative language, character analysis, story mapping

Vocabulary
Definitions, context clues, synonyms/antonyms

Critical Thinking
Evaluating, recalling, supporting details, pros/cons

Writing
Creative writing, point of view, description, narrative, diary, poetry, persuasion, directions, invitation

Across the Curriculum
Social Studies—government, map skills, geography, history, city planning, current events; Math—scale; Art—illustrations, diorama, brochure; Science—erosion, electricity, experiments, biology, technology, life cycles, caves, botany; Drama—skit, oral presentation, script writing; Health—safety, nutrition; Music—composition, lyrics

Genre: science fiction

Setting: fictional, futuristic Ember approximately 241 years after it was built

Point of View: third-person omniscient

Themes: discovering new worlds, following one's dreams, determination, self-reliance

Conflict: person vs. person, person vs. society, person vs. self, person vs. nature

Style: narrative

Tone: suspenseful; mysterious yet hopeful

Date of First Publication: 2003

Summary

The City of Ember takes place in fictional, futuristic Ember—"'the only light in the dark world'" (p. 25)—241 years after the city's creation. The story begins on Assignment Day, when all 12-year-olds randomly select jobs for the next three years. Lina Mayfleet longs to be a messenger, while Doon Harrow aspires to fix Ember's deteriorating generator as a Pipeworks laborer. Over time, supplies and food in Ember have become scarce, and the city now suffers from persistent blackouts. Lina, who struggles to take care of her grandmother and younger sister Poppy, discovers scraps of instructions about how to escape from Ember and turns to Doon for help. Once Doon and Lina discern the Instructions' meaning, they risk their own lives to escape Ember. Along the way, Doon and Lina learn how much they truly value their crumbling city and its citizens.

About the Author

Jeanne DuPrau lives in Menlo Park, California, with her dog, Ethan. Her first fiction novel, *The City of Ember* was so highly acclaimed that it started a bidding war between publishing companies. The novel was named a 2004 ALA Notable Children's Book and was chosen as both a *Kirkus Reviews* Editors' Choice and a New York Public Library's 100 Titles for Reading and Sharing Selection. Prior to her career as a fiction writer, Ms. DuPrau worked as an English teacher, educational publishing editor, and technical writer for Apple, Inc. She has also published six nonfiction books, as well as many essays and short stories. Since *The City of Ember's* debut, Ms. DuPrau has written *The People of Sparks*, its sequel, and most recently, *The Prophet of Yonwood*, its prequel. Ms. DuPrau writes several hours each day and enjoys working in her garden.

Background Information

The city of Ember was built as a last refuge for the human race. When the novel opens more than 200 years after the city's formation, Ember is suffering from shortages of food and medical supplies as well as a deteriorating generator, the city's main power source. Ember's citizens believe Ember is "'the only light in the dark world'" and have no records or memories of life beyond its walls (p. 25). Ember's only light emanates from light bulbs in homes, shops, and street lamps, and because of Ember's problems with the generator, the city suffers from frequent and ever-lengthening blackouts. Due to the intense darkness, people do not venture beyond Ember's borders. A map of Ember at the beginning of the book will help the reader navigate through the city.

Characters

Lina Mayfleet: 12-year-old girl; trades jobs with Doon to become a messenger

Doon Harrow: 12-year-old boy; trades jobs with Lina so he can work underground and fix the city's deteriorating generator; desperately wants to be a hero

Mayor Cole: mayor of Ember; steals food from the city's rations to feed himself

Poppy: Lina's baby sister

Granny: Lina's elderly grandmother

Evaleen Murdo: family friend; cares for Granny, Lina, and Poppy

Clary: Lina's friend; runs the greenhouses; acts as a role model and surrogate parent to Lina

Lizzie Bisco: Lina's best friend; works as a Supply Depot clerk

Looper: Lizzie's boyfriend; steals goods from secret storerooms to sell in his store; delivers stolen food and goods to Mayor Cole

Barton Snode: Assistant Guard to the mayor; kindhearted fellow

Redge Stabmark: Chief Guard to the mayor

Podd Morethwart: former mayor of Ember; distant relative of Granny, Lina, and Poppy's

Captain Fleery: Messenger Captain; Lina's boss

Lister Munk: director of the Pipeworks; Doon's boss

Arlin Froll: girl who works as a Pipeworks laborer

Miss Thorn: Lina and Doon's sixth-grade teacher

Sadge Merrall: Supply Depot clerk; suffers a mental breakdown after he returns from venturing into the Unknown Regions

Loris Harrow: Doon's father; owns the town's Small Items shop; good father to his son, whom he teaches valuable life lessons

Initiating Activities

1. Genre: Have students brainstorm a list of their favorite science-fiction books and/or movies (e.g., *Star Wars*). Discuss characteristics of science fiction based on similarities among items on the list. Compile a class "top ten" list based on the most common books/movies listed.

2. Compare/Contrast: Have students use the Venn Diagram on page 22 of this guide to compare and contrast realistic fiction and science fiction.

3. Prediction: Have students complete the Getting the "Lay of the Land" activity on page 23 of this guide to predict what the novel is about.

4. Social Studies: Divide students into small groups, and instruct each group to plan a city. The city may be set in any time period from present to future. Students must draw a map of the city, decide how the city will be governed, write the city's laws, create a unique name for the city, and describe the conditions under which the city was formed (e.g., peacetime vs. retreat in war, etc.).

5. Math: Instruct students to determine the actual dimensions of Ember based on the scale included in the map at the beginning of the novel.

Vocabulary Activities

1. Figurative Language: Have students look up the definition of "ember." Discuss how an ember burns and students' predictions for how the word may symbolize the book's meaning (e.g., fading, struggling, waiting to reignite, etc.).

2. Glossary: Instruct students to create their own glossaries of difficult or unfamiliar words as they read the novel.

3. Crossword Puzzle: Have each student select ten words from the vocabulary lists in this guide. Have students use the form on page 24 of this guide to create a Crossword Puzzle with the words each has chosen.

The Instructions–Chapter 2

Ember's builders discuss a mysterious box that contains important secrets about the city. The box remains hidden for generations. Over 200 years later, on Assignment Day, Lina wants to be a messenger. Doon, meanwhile, hopes to work in the Pipeworks so he can be near the city's failing generator. When Doon and Lina randomly draw each other's desired jobs, they trade. Lina's curiosity gets her in trouble when she delivers a message to Ember's mayor on her first day of work as a messenger.

Vocabulary
weary
endeavor
anxious
frayed
labyrinth
prosper
generator
trudge
immensely
threadbare
reverberating
resonant
kiosks
serene
antics

Discussion Questions

1. Why do you think the author chooses not to provide the reader with more detail in The Instructions (pp. 1–4)? *(Answers will vary. By not providing more information, the author forces the reader to solve the mystery of Ember's past as he/she reads.)*

2. Do you think it is reasonable for the Builders to insist that the Instructions remain secret for 220 years? Why or why not? *(Answers will vary.)*

3. List the books that Ember students must read. What do you think these titles suggest? *(All students and citizens of Ember must read* The Book of Numbers, The Book of Letters, *and* The Book of the City of Ember. *Answers will vary. Suggestion: None of the books describe life outside of Ember.)*

4. How would you feel if you were required to draw your adult job from a hat? *(Answers will vary.)*

5. How does "messenger" fit Lina's personality better than "Pipeworks laborer"? *(A messenger interacts with people and is amidst action. Lina has an outgoing personality and enjoys being with people. She also loves to run and discover new places and can't stand the idea of being stuck in the dark, cold, damp depths of the underground Pipeworks.)*

6. Do you think it is realistic for Doon to assume that he will be allowed to work on the generator? Why or why not? *(Answers will vary.)*

7. Why does Lina climb on the roof of Town Hall? What does she do on the roof? What does this demonstrate about Lina's personality? *(Lina climbs the Town Hall roof because she is curious. She waves to the people on the streets below. Answers will vary. Suggestion: It shows that Lina is very curious, impulsive, and a bit of a daredevil.)*

8. What does the author mean when she says that "by then [Lina and Doon] had got out of the habit of friendship" (p. 21)? *(When Lina and Doon stopped doing things together as friends, their friendship wasn't as natural as it had once been.)*

9. Do you think the citizens want to leave Ember? Why or why not? *(Answers will vary. Suggestion: No, Ember's citizens are too afraid to leave. They believe that Ember is "'the only light in the dark world'" [p. 25].)*

10. **Prediction:** Does life exist in the Unknown Regions?

Supplementary Activities

1. Prediction: Begin the Prediction Chart on page 25 of this guide. Continue this activity as you read the novel.
2. Character Analysis: Begin the Character Attribute Web for Lina on page 26 of this guide. Continue this activity as you read the novel.
3. Creative Writing: Write three paragraphs in which you describe the Builders' instructions to the citizens of Ember.
4. Art: Based on the author's description on page 24 of the novel, draw a picture of Lina's home.
5. Persuasive Writing: *The Book of the City of Ember* states that "'enough is all that a person of wisdom needs'" (p. 34). Do you agree with this statement? Why or why not? Write a one-page essay in which you attempt to convince someone else of your viewpoint.

Chapters 3–4

On Doon's first day of work at the Pipeworks, he realizes how much Ember's infrastructure has deteriorated. Doon learns that the people who work on the generator do not truly understand how it works; they merely try to keep it running. Lina returns home from work to find Granny in disarray and her baby sister, Poppy, unattended. Lina delivers a message to Clary at the greenhouses; there Lina learns that a new disease is infecting Ember's potato crops. Lina and Clary console Sadge Merrall after he becomes hysterical following a venture into the Unknown Regions.

Vocabulary

anticipation
clamor
throng
chasm
complicated
puzzled
plodding
absolute
gauges
infected

Discussion Questions

1. Do you think it is safe to work in the Pipeworks? What particular safety issues would concern you if you had to work there? *(Answers will vary. Suggestion: It probably is not very safe to work in the Pipeworks. Workers risk falling and/or slipping because of the dark and damp conditions underground.)*

2. How do students learn directions in Ember? Why don't the cardinal directions (e.g., north, south, east, west) relate to anything outside of Ember (e.g., the North or South Pole)? *(Students learn directions based on Ember landmarks. Directions do not relate to anything outside of Ember because the people of Ember do not believe anything else exists.)*

3. In what condition is Ember and its infrastructure? Give examples to support your answer. *(Ember is deteriorating. Food supplies are scarce, and people scour the trash for usable items. The city experiences frequent blackouts due to its failing generator, and Doon believes that Ember's water system is about to break down.)*

4. Explain how Doon has honed his mechanical ability. *(Doon used to take items apart and put them back together. He worked on a watch, faucet, toilet, and refrigerator.)*

5. Describe Granny's state when Lina returns home. *(Granny is panicked and frantically searching the couch cushions for an unknown "lost" item. She doesn't seem to know what she is doing. In recent months, Granny has become forgetful, irresponsible, and increasingly disorganized. She remembers past events but cannot recall recent ones. She likely suffers from an illness such as dementia or Alzheimer's.)*

6. Describe Clary. *(Clary runs the greenhouses. She is shy around people but very comfortable around plants. She is kind and acts like a parent figure to Lina.)*

7. How you would react if you were alone in the Unknown Regions? *(Answers will vary.)*

8. Why do you think there are no flashlights, fire, or matches in Ember? *(Answers will vary.)*

9. Why do you think that the Builders did not equip Ember's citizens with knowledge of how electricity and/or the generator work? Do you think they intended to pass on this knowledge? Why or why not? *(Answers will vary.)*

Supplementary Activities

1. Art: Draw a map of the Pipeworks based on the author's descriptions in Chapter 3.

2. Geography: Most Ember citizens do not understand the concept of a river. Create a guide that describes and explains basic geographic landforms to Ember's citizens. Include landforms that would most likely exist in and around Ember.

3. Figurative Language: Begin the Metaphors and Similes activity on page 27 of this guide. Continue it as you read the novel.

4. Cause/Effect: Begin the Cause/Effect chart on page 28 of this guide. Add to it as you read.

Chapters 5–6

Lina and Poppy visit Looper's shop to buy some colored pencils. While Lina decides on the colors she likes, Poppy wanders out of the shop. Lina's fear of losing Poppy grows as the city of Ember darkens during a seven-minute blackout. Doon finds Poppy and returns her to Lina. Mayor Cole holds a town meeting to reassure Ember's citizens after the lengthy blackout. When Lina returns home from the meeting, she finds Granny busy at work cleaning out the hall closet while Poppy sits in a pile of clutter—including an old box with crumpled pages.

Vocabulary
muddled
wistfully
threaded
spectacle
whimper
tottered
defiant
summon
incoherently
murmur
glinted
incomprehensible
wrenched
chortled

Discussion Questions

1. What do you think the "lost" item that Granny continues to search for actually is? *(Answers will vary.)*

2. Why do you think Ember's citizens take so many vitamins every day? *(Answers will vary. Suggestion: Darkness surrounds Ember, so citizens do not get any vitamin D from sunlight. Also, Ember's limited natural resources prohibit citizens from getting the vitamins they need from food.)*

3. How has Lina been like a mother to Granny and Poppy? Why does Lina relax when Mrs. Murdo is at her home? *(Lina buys food for the family and seems to take care of most household duties. Granny does not seem to be able to take care of daily details, and Poppy needs constant care. When Mrs. Murdo visits, Lina knows she can relax and depend on Mrs. Murdo to take care of things.)*

4. Who are the Believers? In what do you think they believe? *(The Believers are people who gather in the town square to clap and sing. Answers will vary but should include that they believe something is coming to help them.)*

5. How do Ember's colors mirror the city's mood? *(Ember's colors—gray, black, brown, and dark green—are drab and dreary, and people seem to be similarly somber. They do not appear to have social events, athletics, and/or common holidays.)*

6. Discuss what Doon's father means when he says, "The trouble with anger is, it gets hold of you. And then you aren't the master of yourself anymore. Anger is" (p. 89). *(Answers will vary. Suggestion: Doon's father means that an angry person often does or says things he/she doesn't really mean. The anger controls the person, and he/she is unable to control his/her own emotions.)*

7. Describe the box that Poppy finds. What do you think it is, and why do you think it is dented? *(Poppy finds an old box with a hinged lid and damaged lock. Answers will vary but should include that the box is dented because Mayor Morethwart hit it with a hammer.)*

Supplementary Activities

1. Art: Draw Lina's imaginary city as it is described in the novel.

2. Creative Writing: Lina wants the colored pencils so badly that she is ashamed of herself. Write two or three paragraphs in which you describe a time when you wanted something so badly that you were ashamed to admit it.

3. Art: Create a notice for a meeting or an invitation to a party.

Chapters 7–8

Lina asks for Captain Fleery's and Lizzie Bisco's help to decode the message, but neither is interested. Lina sends a message to Mayor Cole about her discovery but receives no response. Realizing that Doon is the only one who will appreciate the magnitude of her discovery, Lina turns to Doon for help. Meanwhile, Doon grows increasingly frustrated by his work at the Pipeworks and inability to understand electricity. Determined to solve Ember's problems, Doon visits the local library to research other ways to create light.

Vocabulary
- pried
- extract
- tattered
- jumble
- frantic
- severe
- eagerly
- illegible
- reluctantly
- recoiling
- enraged
- crevices
- significance

Discussion Questions

1. Why does the note's printing spark Lina's curiosity? *(The printing is small and neat and looks like it was made by a machine. Since there are no computers in Ember, Lina concludes that the writing must have come from the Builders.)*

2. How does Lina know how much time she has left to work after Granny and Poppy are asleep? *(Ember's lights all go out at approximately the same time every night and come on around the same time each morning.)*

3. How would the ability to create movable light change things in Ember? *(The people would have more freedom to move around town and explore the Unknown Regions around Ember.)*

4. Why is it problematic when the storerooms run out of a particular item? *(When the storerooms run out of a particular item, it means that the item is really gone. Ember doesn't have any factories to manufacture new goods.)*

5. Why would it frighten children to see Ember's current storerooms? *(The lack of items in the storerooms would scare children. They would realize how few supplies are left in Ember and would probably worry about what will happen once Ember's remaining supplies are exhausted.)*

6. Do you think Lina should have written the note to Mayor Cole about the Instructions? Why or why not? *(Answers will vary.)*

7. List the phrases Doon learns while reading *Mysterious Words from the Past*, and discuss which element of each phrase is misunderstood. Why do you think these items do not exist or are not discussed in Ember? *("Heavens above": heaven, "Hogwash": hogs, "Batting a thousand": baseball, "All in the same boat": boats; Answers will vary.)*

8. **Prediction:** Will Doon find a way to decrypt the instructions?

Supplementary Activities

1. Creative Thinking: Work in pairs to decode the Instructions that Lina has found (see pp. 94–95 in the novel).

2. Science: Research how light bulbs are made. In an oral report to the class, use household objects to demonstrate the way light bulbs work.

3. Map Skills/Art: Create a blueprint of the storerooms based on the author's description in this section of the novel.

4. Drama: Work in small groups to perform a brief skit in which you demonstrate how anger can have unintended consequences.

5. Science: Conduct a science experiment about erosion.

Chapters 9–10

Lina and Doon determine that the Instructions refer to a locked door in the Pipeworks. While exploring the Pipeworks the next day, Lina and Doon discover another person in the tunnels after work hours. Helplessly, Lina and Doon listen as the mysterious person enters the locked room and then exits. Lina returns home to find Granny ill. Days later, Granny passes away, leaving Lina and Poppy alone.

Vocabulary

self-conscious
mechanism
startled
scuffling
gruff
astonished
ambled
lurking
hoarse
blearily
marvels
methodically
winced

Discussion Questions

1. Why does it surprise Doon that Lina wants to talk to him? *(Lina and Doon have not been friends for several years.)*

2. Why does Lina feel self-conscious when Doon is at her apartment? *(Lina sees her small, crowded apartment through Doon's eyes and worries what he will think.)*

3. How does the blackout change Lina's mind about the severity of Ember's dire situation? *(Lina admits that the length of the blackout has convinced her that Doon was right on Assignment Day, when he told the mayor that Ember is in grave danger.)*

4. To what do you think the locked door in the Pipeworks leads? *(Answers will vary.)*

5. How does the author build suspense as Lina and Doon hear footsteps in the tunnels? *(The author's descriptive language and omniscient point of view allow the reader to experience the situation from Lina and Doon's perspective. The Pipeworks' darkness adds to the suspense, as Lina and Doon do not know who is in the tunnels, where the person is, what he/she is doing, and whether he/she can see them.)*

6. Discuss the mystery person in the Pipeworks. What clues does the author offer about this person's identity? Provide details from the novel to support your answer. *(Answers will vary. Suggestion: The person in the Pipeworks has a "gruff, low voice," long legs, a dark coat, "dark untidy hair," and walks with a "lurching motion that [strikes] Lina as somehow familiar" [p. 129].)*

7. How do you think Lina knows about another city, since other cities are not discussed in Ember? *(Answers will vary. Suggestion: Lina sees visions of the other city in her dreams.)*

8. Why do you think the sky is black in Ember? *(Answers will vary.)*

9. **Prediction:** What will happen to Lina and Poppy?

Supplementary Activities

1. Map Skills: In the novel, Lina and Doon walk from the library across town to Lina's house. Use cardinal directions (e.g., north, east, south, west) and the map in the front of the book to write directions for the route that Lina and Doon take.

2. History: Read Lewis and Clark's account of when they saw the Mississippi River for the first time. Compare and contrast Lewis and Clark's description and Lina's and Doon's comments about the river in the Pipeworks.

3. Figurative Language: List examples of figurative language from this section of the novel. Examples: **Similes**—"breathing…like water gurgling through a clogged pipe" (p. 134), "Taking hold of a pencil was like opening a tap inside her mind through which her imagination flowed" (p. 135), "pressure, like water in a pipe" (p. 135); **Personification**—"The river swallows you and sweeps you away" (p. 127); **Onomatopoeia**—"the chink of a key turning in a lock, and the click of a latch opening" (p. 129); **Metaphor**—door: mystery (p. 131)

4. Persuasive Writing: On page 128 in the novel, Lina comments that the unexpected "ma[kes] things so exciting." Do you agree with her statement? Write a one-page essay in which you explain why or why not.

Chapters 11–12

Lina and Poppy move in with Mrs. Murdo. Lina learns that Lizzie's boyfriend, Looper, has been stealing goods from the storerooms. Lina and Doon discover that the locked door in the Pipeworks opens to Mayor Cole's secret room, which Looper keeps stocked with food and stolen items. Outraged by this injustice, Lina and Doon visit Gathering Hall and tell Barton Snode, one of the mayor's guards, what they have found.

Vocabulary
sternly
gloomier
distracted
astonishment
tainted
sauntering
delectable
beckoned
fiercely
shrill
slogans

Discussion Questions

1. Explain the following statement: "Lina didn't really feel cold but she did feel sad, which was in a way the same" (p. 140). *(Answers will vary. Suggestion: Being cold can make you feel empty and miserable, just like sadness.)*

2. Discuss how the people of Ember feel about each other. Do they seem closer or more distant than people in your community? *(Ember's citizens seem to take care of and look out for each other. Mrs. Murdo steps in to take care of Lina and Poppy even though they are not related to her. Answers will vary.)*

3. Explain the following simile from page 141 of the novel: "The day had a strange but comforting feel to it, like a rest between the end of one time and the beginning of another." *(The day marks the end of Lina's life with Granny and the beginning of her new life with Mrs. Murdo.)*

4. How will life with Mrs. Murdo be different for Lina and Poppy? *(Mrs. Murdo's home is neater, and caring for Lina and Poppy will be less difficult for Mrs. Murdo than it was for Granny and Lina. Previously, Lina was responsible for most household chores and Granny and Poppy's care.)*

5. What taints Lina's enjoyment of the peaches and creamed corn? Why? *(Lina does not enjoy the meal as much since she knows that Looper stole the food from the storerooms.)*

6. Why doesn't Lina take any more food from Lizzie? *(Although she is tempted, Lina thinks it is unfair to take food that does not belong to her. She doesn't like the way it feels to want things so much.)*

7. **Prediction:** What will the guards do with the information about Mayor Cole?

Supplementary Activities

1. Drama: In pairs, act out the scene in which Lina confronts Lizzie about the stolen canned goods (see page 149 in the novel).
2. Persuasive Writing: Lizzie believes that she should be able to eat the stolen food and live well while she can, while Lina thinks it is unfair to eat the stolen goods. Pretend you are either Lina or Lizzie, and write a one-page essay in which you try to convince others of your position.

Chapters 13–14

After talking with Clary, Lina learns that the word "egress" means "exit" and becomes convinced that the Instructions detail an exit from Ember. Lina and Doon use the Instructions to find their way through a tunnel in the Pipeworks. There, they discover candles and matches and learn that they must take a boat down the river to escape the crumbling walls of Ember.

Vocabulary

deciphering
rickety
egress
emerged
urgently
splendid
clarity
realm
plunder
gorging
bewilderment
seize
spurting
surging
threshold
consulted

Discussion Questions

1. Explain the author's description of Lina on page 166 in the novel: "She had had such hopes for that door in the Pipeworks. But hoping so hard had made her jump to conclusions. She'd gone a little too fast. She always went fast. Sometimes it was a good thing and sometimes not." *(Answers will vary. Suggestion: Lina had wanted the Instructions to work so badly that she quickly drew conclusions when she should have slowed down and examined things a bit. Answers will vary.)*

2. How does Clary act as a surrogate parent to Lina? *(Clary listens to Lina's troubles, offers her advice, and keeps her secrets as promised. Lina knows that she can trust Clary and her advice.)*

3. On page 168 in the novel, Clary tells Lina, "Everyone has some darkness inside. It's like a hungry creature. It wants and wants and *wants* with a terrible power. And the more you give it, the bigger and hungrier it gets." Explain what Clary means. Do you think this applies to everyone? *(Clary means that the more power and material gain one accumulates, the more power and material gain they usually want. Answers will vary.)*

4. Compare the sprout to Lina's new life with Mrs. Murdo. *(The sprout is beginning a new life and growing much like Lina, who has started a new life with Poppy and Mrs. Murdo following Granny's death.)*

5. Why does Doon want to keep the information about the Instructions to himself? *(Doon thinks that the guards will announce that he and Lina uncovered the mayor's crimes. Doon wants his father to be surprised by and proud of his accomplishments.)*

6. Do you think that the Builders meant for the "E" on the secret Pipeworks rock to not be readily seen? Why or why not? *(Answers will vary. Suggestion: Yes, to prevent someone from accidentally discovering the secret escape route.)*

7. How do you think Lina and Doon feel as they follow the Instructions into the Pipeworks? *(Answers will vary.)*

8. **Prediction:** Will Lina and Doon take the boat down the river, or will they turn back?

Supplementary Activities

1. Creative Thinking: Create a code, and use it to write a coded message. Switch messages with a partner, and have him/her try to decode the message without help. If the person should need assistance, provide him/her with three clues that will help him/her crack the code and decipher your message.

2. Compare/Contrast: In the novel, Clary describes Mayor Cole as foolish and wicked. Think of another villain in a book you have read, and write a one-page essay in which you compare and contrast that villain and Mayor Cole.

3. Research/Writing: Research and write a report about the Navajo Code Talkers.

4. Sequence: Use the graphic on page 29 to create a Sequence Map of important events that lead to Lina and Doon's discovery of the boat in the underground Pipeworks.

Chapters 15–16

Lina and Doon find an entire room of boats in the Pipeworks and decide to inform Ember's citizens about their discovery at the annual Singing. Before they can do this, though, Lina and Doon learn that the mayor's guards want to arrest them for "spreading vicious rumors" about the mayor. To evade arrest, Lina and Doon hide in the school, where they agree that they must leave Ember on their own. While delivering a note of their intentions to Clary, Lina is arrested and confronted by the mayor. A blackout ensues, and Lina manages to escape.

Vocabulary

desperate
merchandise
generations
feeble
burly
curtly
civic
impudence
accomplice
abundance
majesty
tumult

Discussion Questions

1. Why does Doon want to announce that he and Lina have found an escape route from Ember at the Singing? Do you agree with his reason for wanting to make such an announcement? Why or why not? *(Doon wants to announce his and Lina's discovery at the Singing because he knows everyone in town will attend. The Singing provides a platform for Doon to emerge as a hero. Answers will vary.)*

2. Doon and Lina assume that everyone in Ember will want to journey to an unknown place. Is this a realistic assumption? Do you think that everyone will want to leave Ember? *(Answers will vary. Ember's citizens have been taught that Ember is "the only light in the dark world" [p. 25] so they may be fearful to leave. Others may embrace the option because of Ember's decrepit and disintegrating state.)*

3. Doon realizes that the guards either did not investigate the mayor's secret storeroom or are receiving items from the storerooms as bribes. Which possibility do you think is more realistic? Why? *(Answers will vary.)*

4. Explain what the author means when she says, "[Doon] dashed down the stairs, his anger turning into power for his running feet" (p. 201). *(The author means that Doon's anger propels him to run faster so he can alert Lina that they are in danger.)*

5. Why do you think that the Singing is Ember's only holiday? *(Answers will vary, but most likely the Builders created the annual holiday of the Singing. Ember's original inhabitants probably were not allowed to celebrate other holidays, as this would allude to the existence of other cultures and civilizations beyond Ember.)*

6. How do you think Lina feels when she realizes that Ember is not the only place in the world? *(Answers will vary. Suggestion: Lina probably feels deceived but vindicated, since she constantly dreams about the existence of another city beyond Ember.)*

7. Mayor Cole tells Lina that curiosity is a dangerous, unhealthy, and regrettable quality in a young person. Why does he say this to Lina, and what does he mean? Do you agree with him? Why or why not? *(Mayor Cole says that it is not good to be curious in Ember because times are difficult, and in such times citizens must be loyal, law-abiding, and unquestioning. Mayor Cole uses his position as mayor to rationalize his corrupt behavior. He tells Lina that as mayor he must do what he knows is best for Ember's citizens and implies that the people of Ember do not know what is best. Ember's fate, Mayor Cole explains, depends on its citizens' faith and in what they have been taught about the city. Answers will vary.)*

8. Mayor Cole mentions putting Lina in the "Prison Room." What does this imply about crime in Ember? *(This implies that there is very little crime in Ember. A jail is unnecessary because the city's criminals can all be held in a single room.)*

9. How is the rhythm of "The Song of the River" like a river? Why is it ironic that the citizens sing "The Song of the River"? *("The Song of the River" is low, rolling, and swells like a river's rapids. It is ironic because most citizens have never seen Ember's river, nor do they truly understand what a river is. It is also ironic because the people are oblivious to what Lina and Doon know—that Ember's river is ultimately what will lead them to a new world. Ember's river will prove that Ember is not the only light in the dark world.)*

10. **Prediction:** Will Lina leave with Doon?

Supplementary Activities

1. Oral Presentation: Give a brief oral presentation in which you explain how to use either a boat and paddles or candles and matches. Be sure to include many details and several steps, as though you are speaking to someone who has never before seen or used any of the above items.

2. Creative Writing: On a separate sheet of paper, list three items that you would take with you if you had to flee from home suddenly. For each item, write at least one paragraph in which you explain your reason for choosing that particular item.

3. Science: Research the life cycle of a moth. Based on your findings, draw an illustration that depicts each stage of a moth's life cycle.

4. Music: Based on the author's description on pages 221–223 in the novel, write lyrics to one of the three songs of Ember ("The Song of the City," "The Song of the River," or "The Song of Darkness").

Chapters 17–18

Unaware that Lina has freed herself from the guards, Doon wonders whether he should continue on his journey alone or stay behind to help Lina. Doon leaves a note for his father on the public bulletin board and then makes his way to the Pipeworks. Lina meets him outside the front entrance, carrying Poppy on her back. Doon and Lina cling to Poppy as they maneuver their rowboat down the river. Along a path at the river's end, Poppy finds a diary, which Lina and Doon agree to read later. As the trio ascends up the rock path and away from the river, Lina realizes that, amidst her arrest, she forgot to give Clary the note that explains how to locate Ember's escape route.

Vocabulary

dread
harmonies
dispersing
queasy
hoisted
rungs
hostile
tether
churning
plunged
shrieking
gleefully

Discussion Questions

1. Why is it ironic that Doon's name appears on posters all around Ember? *(It is ironic because Doon had hoped that exposing the Mayor's corruption would make him a famous hero. Presently, it has only made him an infamous criminal.)*

2. Do you think someone will deliver the note to Doon's father? Why or why not? Do you think the same is true in most communities? Explain your answer. *(Answers will vary. Suggestions: It probably would not be delivered in most communities. In Ember, however, it is likely that someone will deliver the message. Ember seems to be a closely-knit society in which citizens know, care about, and look after each other.)*

3. Do you agree with Lina's decision to bring Poppy along on the journey out of Ember? Why or why not? What would you have done in the same situation? *(Answers will vary. Some students may agree with Lina's decision to bring Poppy along and say that it will provide both sisters with much needed security. Students may also say that by bringing Poppy, Lina will no longer have to worry about her inability to see Poppy again and/or the effect her absence will have on Poppy's well-being. Other students may disagree with Lina's decision and say that Poppy could be hurt, especially since Lina does not know where they are going and/or whether it will be safe.)*

4. How do you know that the Builders carefully planned Ember's escape route? *(Answers will vary. Suggestion: The Builders accounted for each item that one would need to escape from Ember [e.g., candles and matches to see in the dark, rungs to climb down onto the embankment, a tether to lower the boat into the river, a hook to hold the boat in place amidst the river's current, etc.]. Additionally, the Builders discreetly positioned all of the items so that no one would find them unless he/she knew what to look for.)*

5. How far do you think Lina, Doon, and Poppy travel on the river? Use details from the book to support your answer. *(Answers will vary.)*

6. Who do you think left the diary along the path? *(Answers will vary. Suggestion: One of Ember's first settlers probably left the diary.)*

7. Why does Lina believe that Ember is unsafe? *(Ember's situation is very unpredictable due to the problems with the generator as well as the lack of supplies.)*

8. **Prediction:** Where does the path lead?

9. **Prediction:** Will Ember's other citizens find the escape route?

Supplementary Activities
1. Music: Select a song that describes where you live. Include the song's lyrics, and explain how they represent your community.
2. Creative Writing: Write a one-page narrative in which you describe the events of this section from Poppy's point of view.
3. Creative Writing: Write five diary entries which could be included in the diary Poppy finds.
4. Art/Science: Create a brochure that advertises a tour through a cave. Include how the cave was formed, as well as landforms, rock formations, and animals that tourists may encounter.

Chapters 19–20

Doon, Lina, and Poppy climb several hours to reach the opening of what they eventually learn is a cave. They emerge from the dark pathways only to find themselves surrounded by more darkness—except for the moon and stars' faint glow—as they have arrived on the earth's surface during nightfall. A few hours later, they witness their first sunrise, along with several other of Earth's wonders. As they read the journal left behind in the cave tunnel, Lina and Doon learn that the Builders created Ember as a safe haven from world disaster. While exploring a field, Lina, Doon, and Poppy discover another opening to the cave and decide to enter. As they peer down into the darkness, they see the dim lights of Ember, nestled at the bottom of a deep chasm. Lina removes the note to Clary from her pocket and adds a few lines about their discovery—a new land with light in the sky—before tying it up in Doon's shirt. Lina tosses the shirt, weighed down by a rock, into the depths below. Mrs. Murdo, while walking down the street, sees a strange bundle fall from the sky and reaches down to pick it up.

Vocabulary
refugees
relentlessly
infinitely
vast
billowed
crimson
seeped
trill
catastrophes
pondered
gullies

Discussion Questions
1. Do you believe Lina is naïve to think that people anxiously await her, Doon, and Poppy's arrival and will be at the surface to welcome them? Why do you think Lina believes this? *(Answers will vary. Some students may say that Lina is naïve to think such a thing. Others may argue that Lina isn't naïve but merely a 12-year-old child who doesn't realize that people on Earth's surface aren't aware that Ember exists.)*

2. Lina says the new world feels familiar and that she may have dreamed about it. Do you think this is possible? Why or why not? *(Answers will vary.)*

3. Why weren't Ember's first inhabitants allowed to bring books or photographs with them? *(The Builders insisted that there could not be any record of an existing world beyond Ember.)*

4. What do you think happened on Earth that spurred scientists to create Ember? *(Answers will vary, but most likely an impending nuclear war.)*

5. Do you agree with the restrictions the Builders placed on Ember's first citizens? Why or why not? *(Answers will vary. Most students will probably disagree with the restrictions and argue that a person should not be stripped of his/her possessions or banned from discussing memories of his/her previous life. However, some students might mention that the Builders' restrictions were necessary, given the purpose of Ember's creation. The Builders created Ember as a refuge for the human race; the city was designed to ensure the survival of human beings in the advent of global disaster.)*

6. The diary's author knew that she was going to have to live underground. How would you feel about this? List the pros and cons of living underground. *(Answers will vary. Students may mention the benefit of being unaffected by warfare and/or diseases on earth. They may also discuss the difficulty and dreariness of life without sunshine.)*

7. How do Doon, Lina, and Poppy most likely look? What would you think if they had approached you and explained that they traveled to earth from an underground city? *(Answers will vary. Suggestions: Doon, Lina, and Poppy probably look pale and sickly. They have never been exposed to sunlight, so their skin is most likely very white and sensitive. Because most foods cannot grow in Ember due to the absence of sunlight, and because the people of Ember have not built factories to produce food, citizens mainly eat small quantities of vegetables. Poppy, Doon, and Lina probably look scrawny and malnourished due to the lack of meat and protein in their diets.)*

8. **Prediction:** What will Mrs. Murdo do with the note?

Supplementary Activities

1. Research/Geography: Research areas of the world with large refugee populations, and label these locations on a world map. Write a caption that explains where the refugees came from and why.

2. Science: Explore the life cycle of plants and trees. Create a diagram in which you explain this cycle to someone who has never before seen a plant or tree.

3. Descriptive Writing: Write a descriptive essay about a sunrise as though you are witnessing one for the first time.

4. Creative Writing: Pretend you are one of Ember's original inhabitants. Write three diary entries—each at least one paragraph long—in which you describe your first week at Ember.

Post-reading Discussion Questions

1. Select a character that changes from the beginning to the end of the novel. How does this character change? Do you think he/she changes for the better? Why or why not? *(Answers will vary.)*

2. What is one lesson that Lina learns? *(Answers will vary but should include that Lina learns the importance of following her dreams and trusting another person.)*

3. What are the main messages the author conveys throughout the novel? Provide examples from the novel to support your answer. *(Answers will vary but could include discovering new worlds, following one's dreams, self-reliance, and/or determination.)*

4. How is this novel a work of science fiction? *(The novel is a fictional story that occurs at some point in the future. The city of Ember was created by accomplished scientists, and its people depend on technology [e.g., the generator] to survive.)*

5. Would you recommend this novel to a friend? Why or why not? *(Answers will vary.)*

6. Select a character from the story that reminds you of someone you know. How and why does the character remind you of this person? *(Answers will vary.)*

7. Select a part of the novel that you would like to change. How and why would you like to change it? *(Answers will vary.)*

8. Did the novel end as you had expected? If not, how did the ending differ from your expectations? *(Answers will vary.)*

9. What do you think is the single most important event in the novel? Provide details from the novel to support your answer. *(Answers will vary. Suggestion: Poppy's discovery of the message could be considered most important because it allowed the rest of the story to occur. If Poppy hadn't found the piece of paper inside the box, Lina wouldn't have found the Instructions, and she and Doon wouldn't have found a way to escape from Ember.)*

10. Which character from the novel did you like best? Which did you like least? Explain your answer. *(Answers will vary.)*

Post-reading Extension Activities

Writing

1. Create a time line of the events in the novel. Include small illustrations next to each event on the time line.
2. Write a review of the novel. Include whether you would recommend the novel to a friend and the reason for your choice.
3. Pretend you are Lina, and write a poem in which you convey your feelings about leaving Ember.

Reading

1. Read *The People of Sparks*, the sequel to *The City of Ember*. Compare and contrast the two novels.
2. Read *The Prophet of Yonwood*, the prequel to *The City of Ember*. Compare and contrast the two novels.

Art

1. Create a diorama of an important scene in the novel.
2. Create a guide to the earth's surface for Ember refugees. Include information relevant to daily survival (e.g., edible foods found in the wild, insects and animals to avoid, dangerous weather patterns, etc.).
3. Create a flip book that depicts an important event from the novel.

Drama

1. Rewrite your favorite scene from the novel in script form. With a group of classmates, perform the scene for your class.

History

1. Research bomb shelters of the past and present. Contrast their methods of construction and supplies that past and present shelters include.

Assessment for *The City of Ember*

Assessment is an ongoing process. The following eight items can be completed during the novel study. Once finished, the student and teacher will check the work. Points may be added to indicate the level of understanding.

Name _____ Date _____

Student	Teacher	
_____	_____	1. List five to ten examples of figurative language found in the novel. Identify the literary device used in each.
_____	_____	2. Write a summary of *The City of Ember* using at least ten vocabulary words.
_____	_____	3. Complete one of the Post-reading Extension Activities listed on page 20 of this guide, and share with the class.
_____	_____	4. Correct all quizzes and tests taken over the novel.
_____	_____	5. Select two characters from the novel to compare and contrast. (Note: You may use either Lina or Doon as one of the characters, but you may not use both.).
_____	_____	6. Create a book jacket for the novel.
_____	_____	7. Write five review questions about the novel. Exchange questions with a partner, and answer each other's review questions.
_____	_____	8. Complete the Story Map on page 30 of this guide.

Venn Diagram

Directions: Use the Venn diagram below to compare and contrast characteristics of realistic fiction and science fiction.

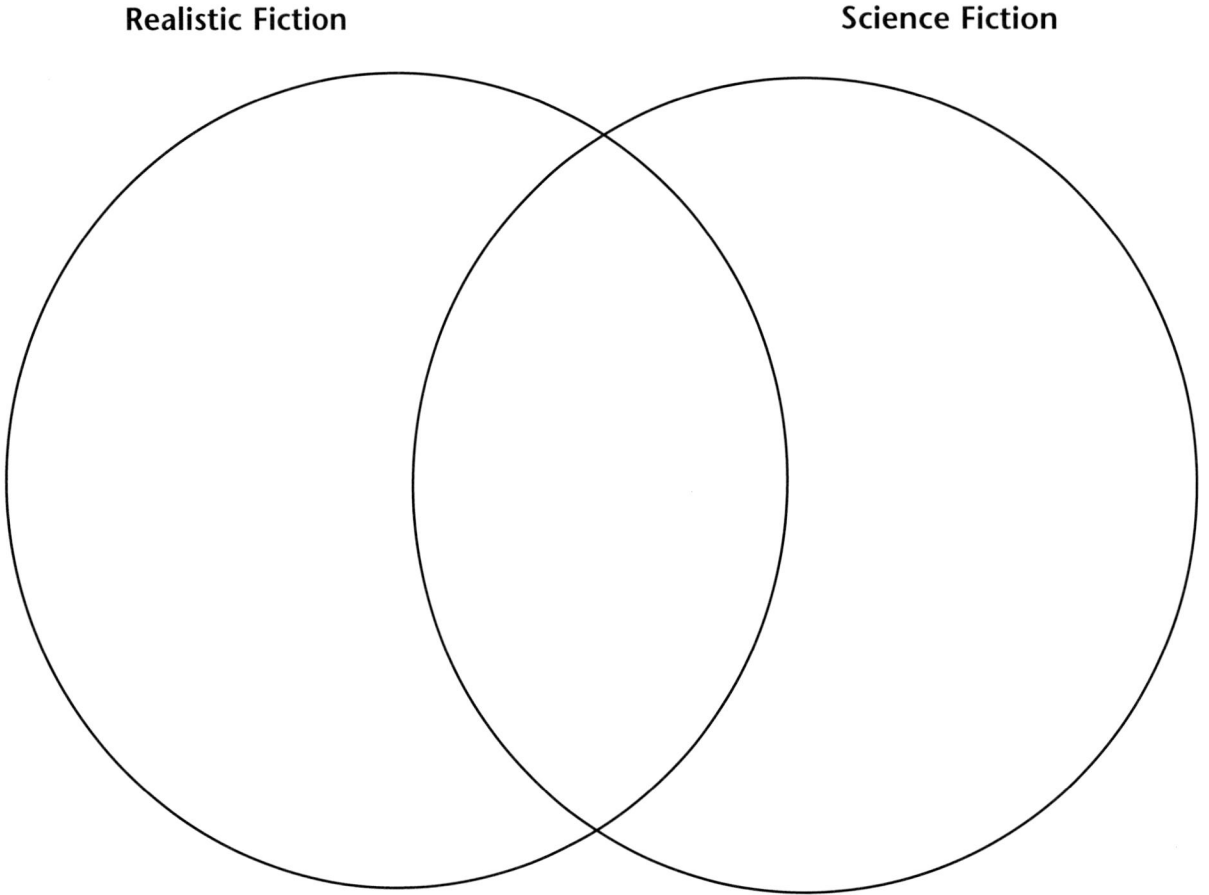

Getting the "Lay of the Land"

Directions: Prepare for reading by answering the following short-answer questions.

1. Who is the author?
   _____

2. What does the title suggest to you about the book?
   _____
   _____
   _____
   _____

3. When was the book first copyrighted?
   _____

4. How many pages are there in the book?
   _____

5. Thumb through the book. Read three pages—one from near the beginning, one from near the middle, and one from near the end. What predictions can you make about the book?
   _____
   _____
   _____
   _____
   _____

6. What does the cover suggest to you about the book?
   _____
   _____
   _____
   _____

Crossword Puzzle

Directions: Select ten vocabulary words from the vocabulary lists found in this guide. Create a crossword puzzle answer key by filling in the grid below. Be sure to number the squares for each word. Blacken any spaces not used by the letters. Then, write clues to the crossword puzzle. Number the clues to match the numbers in the squares. The teacher will give each student a blank grid. Make a blank copy of your crossword puzzle for other students to answer. Exchange your clues with someone else, and solve the blank puzzle s/he gives you. Check the completed puzzles with the answer keys.

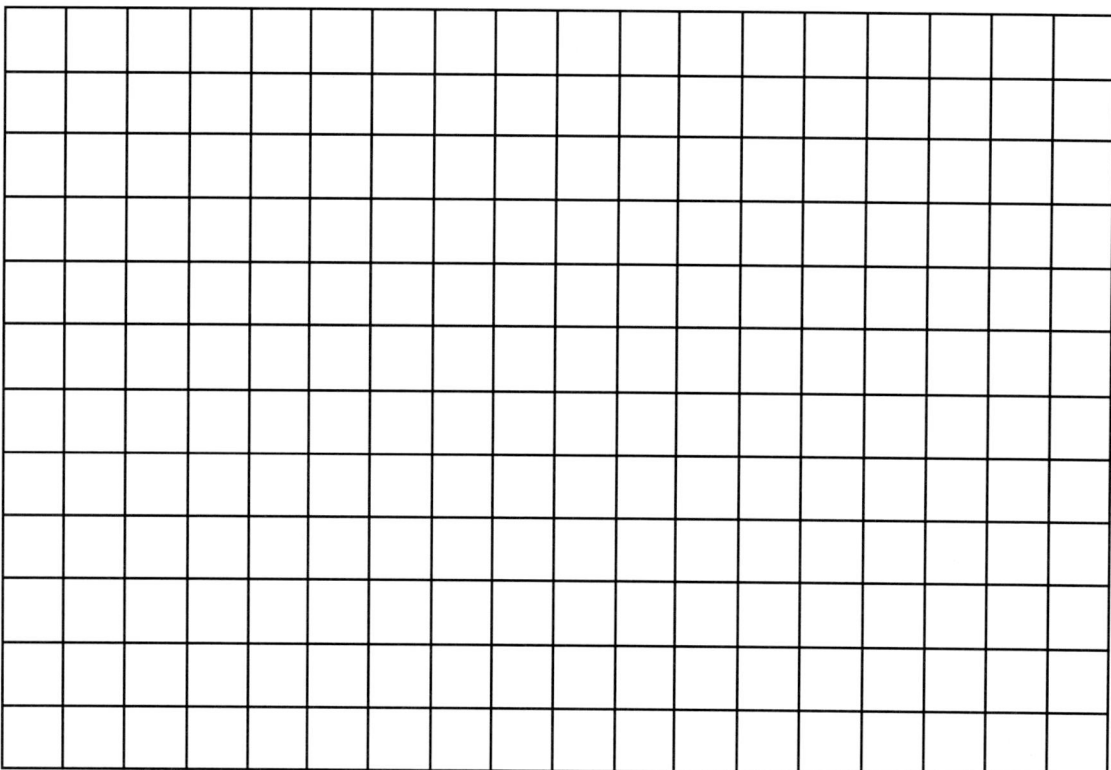

Prediction Chart

What characters have we met so far?	What is the conflict in the story?	What are your predictions?	Why did you make these predictions?

Character Attribute Web

Directions: Complete the attribute web below for Lina Mayfleet. Fill in the blanks with words and phrases that tell how Lina acts and looks, as well as what she says and feels.

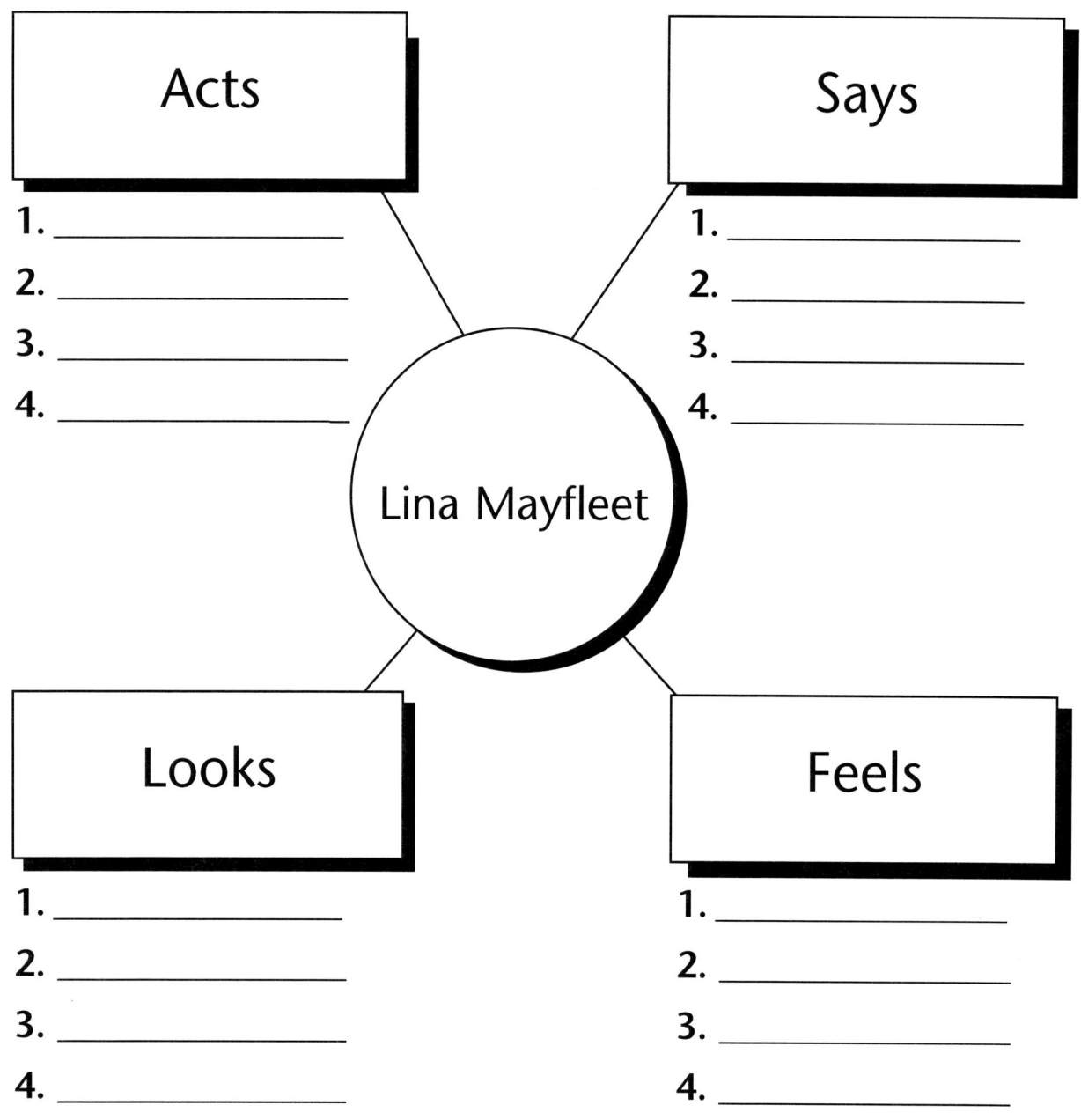

Metaphors and Similes

A **metaphor** is a comparison between two unlike objects. For example, "he was a human tree." A **simile** is a comparison between two unlike objects that uses the words *like* or *as*. For example, "the color of her eyes was like the cloudless sky."

Directions: Complete the chart below by listing metaphors and similes from the novel, as well as the page numbers on which they are found. Identify metaphors with an "M" and similes with an "S." Translate the comparisons in your own words, and then list the objects being compared.

Metaphors/Similes	Ideas/Objects Being Compared
1. Translation:	
2. Translation:	
3. Translation:	

Cause/Effect

Directions: To plot cause and effect in a story, first list the sequence of events. Then mark causes with a C and effects with an E. Sometimes in a chain of events, one item may be both a cause and an effect. Draw arrows from cause statements to the appropriate effects.

Events in the story	Cause	Effect
1.		
2.		
3.		
4.		
5.		
6.		
7.		
8.		
9.		
10.		

Another way to map cause and effect is to look for an effect and then backtrack to the single or multiple causes.

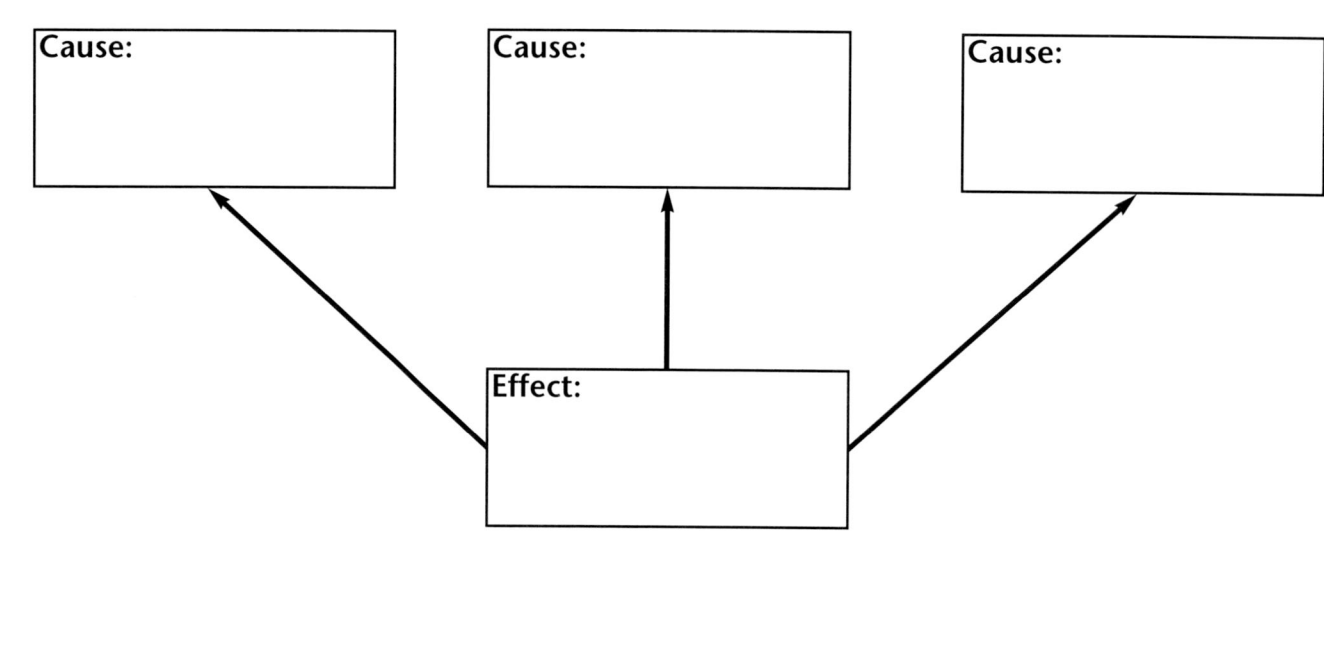

Sequence Map

Directions: In the novel, Lina and Doon take many steps to reach the boat in the Pipeworks. Choose five events that lead to Lina and Doon's discovery of the boat, and put them sequentially into the flow chart. Instead of writing a description of each event, draw a small illustration in each of the boxes below.

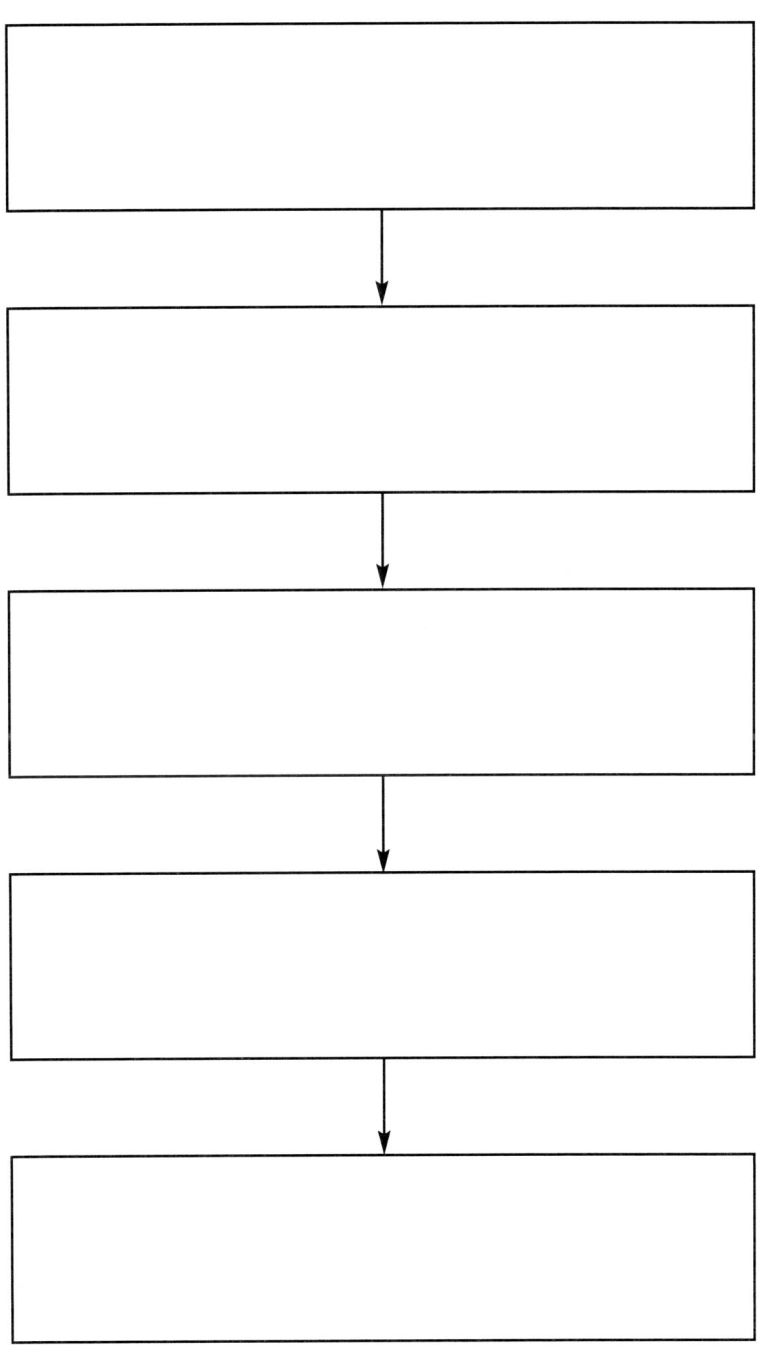

Story Map

Directions: Complete the story map below using information from the novel.

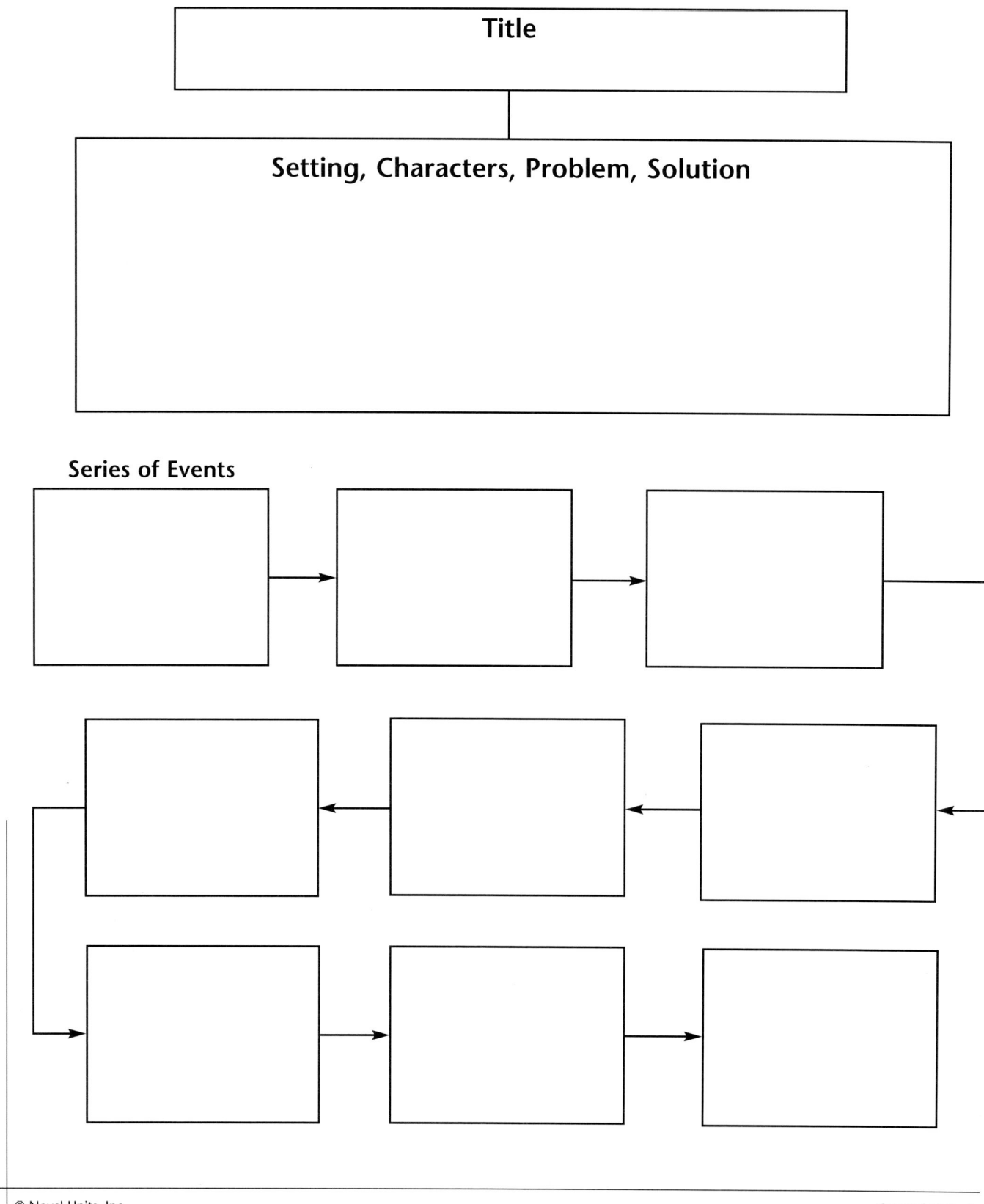

Linking Novel Units® Lessons to National and State Reading Assessments

During the past several years, an increasing number of students have faced some form of state-mandated competency testing in reading. Many states now administer state-developed assessments to measure the skills and knowledge emphasized in their particular reading curriculum. The discussion questions and post-reading questions in this Novel Units® Teacher Guide make excellent open-ended comprehension questions and may be used throughout the daily lessons as practice activities. The rubric below provides important information for evaluating responses to open-ended comprehension questions. Teachers may also use scoring rubrics provided for their own state's competency test.

Please note: The Novel Units® Student Packet contains optional open-ended questions in a format similar to many national and state reading assessments.

Scoring Rubric for Open-Ended Items

3-Exemplary	Thorough, complete ideas/information Clear organization throughout Logical reasoning/conclusions Thorough understanding of reading task Accurate, complete response
2-Sufficient	Many relevant ideas/pieces of information Clear organization throughout most of response Minor problems in logical reasoning/conclusions General understanding of reading task Generally accurate and complete response
1-Partially Sufficient	Minimally relevant ideas/information Obvious gaps in organization Obvious problems in logical reasoning/conclusions Minimal understanding of reading task Inaccuracies/incomplete response
0-Insufficient	Irrelevant ideas/information No coherent organization Major problems in logical reasoning/conclusions Little or no understanding of reading task Generally inaccurate/incomplete response

Notes